ENGINEERING
THE SPACE
NEEDLE

BY KATE CONLEY

CONTENT CONSULTANT
Tyler S. Sprague
Assistant Professor, Department of Architecture
University of Washington

Cover image: The Space Needle is a brightly lit feature
of the Seattle, Washington, skyline.

Core Library

An Imprint of Abdo Publishing
abdopublishing.com

abdopublishing.com

Published by Abdo Publishing, a division of ABDO, PO Box 398166, Minneapolis, Minnesota 55439. Copyright © 2018 by Abdo Consulting Group, Inc. International copyrights reserved in all countries. No part of this book may be reproduced in any form without written permission from the publisher. Core Library™ is a trademark and logo of Abdo Publishing.

Printed in the United States of America, North Mankato, Minnesota
092017
012018

Cover Photo: Shutterstock Images
Interior Photos: Shutterstock Images, 1, 34–35; Art Wager/iStockphoto, 4–5, 45; AP Images, 7, 19; Detlev van Ravenswaay/Science Source, 9; Thomas Kienzle/AP Images, 11; Bettmann/Getty Images, 14–15; Seattle Engineering Department/Seattle Municipal Archives, 21; Miscellaneous Prints/Seattle Municipal Archives, 24–25; City Light Photographic Negatives/Seattle Municipal Archives, 28, 29, 43; Red Line Editorial, 32; Jeffrey M. Frank/Shutterstock Images, 39

Editor: Arnold Ringstad
Imprint Designer: Maggie Villaume
Series Design Direction: Laura Polzin

Publisher's Cataloging-in-Publication Data

Names: Conley, Kate, author.
Title: Engineering the Space Needle / by Kate Conley.
Description: Minneapolis, Minnesota : Abdo Publishing, 2018. | Series: Building by design | Includes online resources and index.
Identifiers: LCCN 2017946986 | ISBN 9781532113772 (lib.bdg.) | ISBN 9781532152658 (ebook)
Subjects: LCSH: Space Needle (Seattle, Wash.)--Juvenile literature. | Towers--Design and construction--Juvenile literature. | Washington (State)--Seattle--Juvenile literature. | Building--Juvenile literature.
Classification: DDC 725.9709--dc23
LC record available at https://lccn.loc.gov/2017946986

CONTENTS

A SEATTLE LANDMARK

Every day, Valeriy Palanchuk clips himself into a harness. Then he steps out onto a narrow, sloped ring. It is known as the halo. This metal ledge circles the Space Needle, a tower in Seattle, Washington. It is almost 600 feet (183 m) off the ground. Palanchuk walks gracefully around it. Tourists inside the tower wave to him.

Palanchuk works at the Space Needle. He and other workers brave frightening heights. They plant flags on the top. They replace the airplane beacon and light bulbs on top of the tower when they burn out. All their work keeps the tower safe and ready for visitors.

The Space Needle attracts visitors from around the globe.

It is hard for people in Seattle to remember the city before the Space Needle. The landmark is recognized around the world. But it had a humble beginning. It was inspired by a fair, a satellite, and a television tower.

A WORLD'S FAIR

In 1955 Washington State lawmakers set up a special committee. Its task was to explore the idea of hosting a World's Fair. These fairs are gatherings for people across the globe. They showcase new inventions and different cultures. Such fairs usually last several months. Hosting one is a great honor.

Edward E. Carlson led the committee. He knew it was a large project. The fair would bring millions of visitors to the state. Many would be coming from other countries. The fair would have to provide gardens, entertainment, museums, and exhibit halls.

The committee had to think about many elements. It had to pick a host city. It also had to pick a theme that would interest people. The committee had to find a site

The World's Fair held in New York City in 1939 featured its own striking architecture.

to build the fairgrounds. It had to figure out how to pay for all this too.

Critics slowed the process. They worried about crowds. And no one had come up with an inspiring theme. The committee seemed stuck. It lacked a clear direction. And it had trouble finding money and property.

FAMOUS FAIR STRUCTURES

Host cities for World's Fairs often created structures that amazed visitors. In London, England, the Crystal Palace awed visitors at the 1851 fair. It was an exhibit hall made entirely of glass and iron. In Paris, France, Gustave Eiffel built an elegant iron tower as the entrance to the 1889 fair. The Eiffel Tower soon became a symbol of Paris. Visitors to the 1893 World's Fair lined up to ride the world's first Ferris wheel in Chicago, Illinois. Today, Ferris wheels can be found at carnivals and amusement parks across the world.

INSPIRED BY *SPUTNIK*

Then, in 1957, everything changed. On October 4, the Soviet Union launched *Sputnik*. It was the world's first satellite. Its launch marked the beginning of space exploration. The future of space travel and science interested people across the world. The committee realized this would be a popular theme.

The committee moved forward with this idea. The fair became known as the Century 21 Exposition. Its theme was "Man in the Space Age." Exhibits would

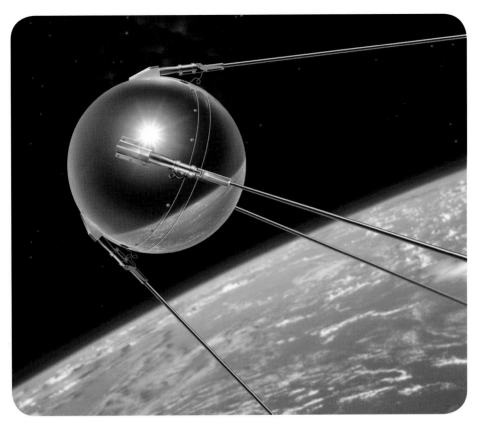

The launch of *Sputnik* kicked off the space age and gave the fair planners their theme.

feature life in the twenty-first century. Future homes, fashions, and offices would be on display. Other exhibits would highlight advances in space and science.

THE STUTTGART TOWER

The only thing missing for the fair was an impressive structure to be its symbol. But Carlson had an idea.

He traveled to West Germany in 1959. There he visited the new Stuttgart Tower. It was the world's first television tower. The concrete column reached 712 feet (217 m) into the air. Visitors could take an elevator to the top. There they could dine and enjoy amazing views.

The Stuttgart Tower left a powerful impression on Carlson. Inspired by it, he drew a sketch of a new tower. It was a tall column with a ring at the top. Under his drawing he wrote the words *Space Needle*.

Carlson soon returned to the United States. He followed up on his Space Needle idea. Other officials liked it. A tower pointing to space seemed perfect. It would make an impression on visitors. And it would go along with the fair's theme. Architects and engineers refined the design. Building began in April 1961, and the tower opened a year later.

The Stuttgart Tower provided inspiration for the Space Needle.

GROWING EXCITEMENT

Jay Rockey oversaw public relations for the fair. One of his jobs was to generate excitement about the fair so people would come to it. The Space Needle made his job easy. "As the Space Needle went up into the air, the intensity of our ticket sales went up with it," recalled Rockey. "This was a big project. It wasn't just building a building, it was building a structure that hadn't been done like this before. By the time the steel got to the top, we were really in gear. We knew then that we were going to make it."

A LASTING SUCCESS

The Century 21 Exposition opened on April 21, 1962. In the next six months, nearly 10 million people visited it. The fair was an outstanding success. When it ended, Seattle had proven itself as an exciting city of the future. It had also gained a new city landmark in Carlson's mighty tower.

The Space Needle quickly became a symbol of the city. People used it as a reference point. It became the site of weddings and parachute jumps. Actors filmed movies there, and musicians used it as a concert site.

The idea that had begun as a sketch did not happen overnight. Experts were not sure such a tower could be built safely. The site was very small for such a large tower. And the deadline was short. The planning and building would have to be done in just over a year. It was a job that required skill, determination, and steady nerves.

EXPLORE ONLINE

Chapter One explores how the Space Needle changed the landscape in Seattle. Read the article at the link below to trace the history of observation decks across the world. What is the biggest difference you notice between early towers and later towers? What might account for this change?

OBSERVATION DECKS
abdocorelibrary.com/engineering-space-needle

DESIGNING THE SPACE NEEDLE

The idea of the Space Needle excited fair planners. But Carlson's design was only a rough sketch. It was much too simple for anyone to use as a building plan. Carlson turned to architect John Graham and his team for help in refining the design. He instructed them to use their imaginations.

Graham's architects explored many ideas for how people would use the structure during the fair and after it. One design included a planetarium, an aquarium, and

The planners would go through several revisions and refinements before arriving at the final design.

a revolving restaurant. Another design had a radar antenna for sending signals to the moon. Architects even considered putting a helicopter landing pad on the tower's top.

The ideas were certainly creative. They were also costly and impractical to build. But one idea stuck with Graham: the revolving restaurant. Graham had just designed one for a mall in Honolulu, Hawaii. He thought it could work on the Space Needle too.

Graham asked his architects to continue with this idea. He wanted the restaurant to look like a saucer perched on a tall shaft. The shaft on early designs was thick and ugly. Revised plans used a cage and cables to support a slender shaft. But it was not as elegant as Graham had imagined.

STEINBRUECK'S INFLUENCE

In the summer of 1960, Graham hired Victor Steinbrueck to draw some new designs. He made many sketches of the tower. None of them seemed quite right. Then one day a small wooden sculpture in his office sparked an idea for the tower.

The sculpture was an abstract piece called "The Feminine One." It was a female form reaching for the sky. She had a narrow waist and long, graceful limbs. The statue's simple lines lent themselves easily to the tower's form. Using this as inspiration would transform the tower into a large-scale, elegant work of art.

PERSPECTIVES

"THE 550-FOOT HIGH WHITE ELEPHANT"

Joseph Gandy was president of Seattle's World's Fair. He asked the city to help pay for the Space Needle. Gandy said it would be "one of the greatest tourist attractions in any metropolitan civic center area." But city leaders refused. They feared it would be a gimmick. They did not want to be responsible for it. Seattle's superintendent of buildings, Fred McCoy, called it the "550-foot [168-m] high white elephant." Gandy eventually found private investors. Today, the Space Needle is still owned and operated privately.

Steinbrueck spent the weekend working on his new design. It had three legs that surrounded a shaft. They narrowed about two-thirds of the way up. Then they flared out again to support the revolving restaurant on top. Steinbrueck showed the design to Graham and his team the following Monday. They loved it. The Space Needle had finally found its form.

ENGINEERING CHALLENGES

With a design in hand, officials needed a structural engineer. Early engineering studies were done by the John Graham Company. The company designed much of the structure. But the officials still needed to hire an expert to finalize the design. They hired John Minasian for the job in February 1961. He had a huge task. Within just 14 months, Minasian would need to complete all the tests and calculations to make the Space Needle safe. Strong winds and earthquakes were his biggest concerns.

THE FINAL
DESIGN

An elevation drawing is a tool used by engineers and architects. It shows a two-dimensional image of what the completed building will look like. Important measurements are labeled, as well as the major elements of the building. Some of these measurements and elements are overlaid on this photo of the completed building. What role do you think an elevation drawing plays in planning a building?

Aircraft warning beacon

83.5 feet (25.5 m)

Observation level

18.75 feet (5.72 m)

Restaurant level

602.25 feet (183.57 m)

300 feet (91 m)

Platform 2

100 feet (30.5 m)

Platform 1

100 feet (30.5 m)

Plaza level

19

Wind speeds increase with elevation. A light breeze at the base of the Space Needle could be a strong wind at the top. Minasian knew the wind's force would push against the tower. This is called wind load. It could make the top of the tower sway. If it swayed too much, the tower could become unsafe.

Earthquakes were another challenge in the tower's design. Seattle's location on the west coast means it is at risk for large earthquakes. An earthquake could shake the tower violently. This could force the tower to slide away from its foundation or even topple. To prevent this, Minasian built a massive foundation for the Space Needle.

FINDING A SITE

The team working on the Space Needle did not have many options for a building site. Legal restrictions left them only one option right on the fairgrounds. The site was a square only 120 feet (36.6 m) on each side. It was a tiny piece of land for a tower that would rise 605 feet (184 m). But Minasian's deep, strong foundation made it work.

A strong foundation and base would keep the tall, thin Space Needle steady.

A STRONG FOUNDATION

The foundation Minasian designed was shaped like the letter Y. Each leg of the Y would support one leg of the Space Needle. The foundation would be

30 feet (9 m) deep. It would be filled with concrete and steel reinforcing bars. Huge anchor bolts would secure the tower to the foundation.

This arrangement lowered the tower's center of gravity, the average location of its overall mass. Without the foundation, the Space Needle's center of gravity would be approximately halfway up the tower. This would make the tower unstable in high winds and earthquakes. But the deep, heavy foundation shifted the center of gravity to five feet (1.5 m) above the ground. This would make the tower much more stable.

Minasian tested the design before building began. He took a model of the Space Needle to a wind tunnel. It simulated high winds and earthquakes. Results showed the design was stable and strong. The Space Needle exceeded the 1962 wind and earthquake building codes. Building on the tower could now begin. It would be a race against time to complete the tower before the opening day of the fair.

STRAIGHT TO THE
SOURCE

Rod Kirkwood was involved in all the engineering aspects of the Space Needle, from pouring the foundation to erecting the tower. When he reflected on it years later, he said:

> We put enough concrete foundation under [the Space Needle] so that—if you discount the dirt that's underneath it—the center of gravity is a few feet above ground—not too much more above the ground than the top of your head. So the possibility of tipping it over is pretty remote. That was part of the reason for pouring all that concrete; part of it was [also] to make sure there wasn't any deflection in the foundation. If we'd deflected one leg more than another, we would have had the 'leaning tower of Seattle.'

> Source: Robert Spector. *Symbol of Seattle: The Space Needle*. Seattle, WA: Documentary Media, 2006. Print. 52.

Changing Minds

Imagine someone believed that a tower as tall and slim as the Space Needle could never be truly safe. What evidence in Kirkwood's quote could you use to change his or her mind? What makes Kirkwood's quote convincing?

BUILDING THE NEEDLE

On April 17, 1961, a collection of huge machinery descended upon the Space Needle site. Power shovels, bulldozers, and dump trucks quickly began work. For the next 11 days, they dug the foundation Minasian had designed.

Next, workers filled the hole with 250 tons (227 metric tons) of steel reinforcing bars. This material is often called rebar. It gives the concrete added strength. When this was complete, workers added 72 bolts. Each one was 30 feet (9 m) long. The bolts would anchor the tower legs to the foundation.

The tower rose quickly as the date of the fair approached.

At last the site was ready for concrete. At 5:00 a.m. on May 26, concrete trucks arrived on the site. As many as eight trucks rolled into place at a time. Each one poured its load and left, with another truck waiting to take its place. Crowds gathered to watch the event.

By 5:00 p.m., the foundation was complete. In only 12 hours, 467 truckloads of concrete had been poured. The concrete, rebar, and bolts formed a mighty foundation. It weighed a whopping 5,850 tons (5,307 metric tons). This was more than the Space

Needle itself. The massive foundation kept the tower's center of gravity low.

RAISING THE TOWER

With the pour complete, the crowds left. They would have to wait a while longer before the tower would begin to rise. For the next month, little changed at the site. The concrete had to harden before any further building could take place.

In late June, construction boss Paul Collop directed his crews to begin building. Thirty-nine welders joined sections of steel to form the core. Meanwhile, other workers set 22-ton (20–metric ton) pedestals into place on the steel anchor bolts. They would support each of the tower's three massive legs.

As the core continued to rise, work on the legs began. On July 19, workers put the first leg section into place. It was not a small task. Each section was 90 feet (27 m) long and weighed 50 tons (45 metric tons). Workers joined the sections using bolts and welds.

Through the late summer, workers continued to build up the tower's steel structure.

Inspectors checked the work each night. They x-rayed the welds to make sure the joints were strong.

REACHING HIGHER

Each leg was made up of two steel columns. The long columns gave the tower strength. They also allowed it to rise quickly. By midsummer, the tower reached a height of 120 feet (37 m). While this was great news, it also posed a problem. The cranes on the ground could no longer reach the top of the tower.

With ground cranes no longer an option, Collop had to be creative. He designed a crane that sat inside the core. The crane's long arm reached over the core

The tower itself served as a support structure as the workers and machinery reached new heights.

and down to the ground. There, it picked up a section of leg or core and lifted it.

Next, workers welded the new piece into place. The crane would then ride up the newly built section. Then workers repeated the process of building a section and raising the crane. It allowed the crane to bring heavy supplies all the way to the highest parts of the tower.

BENDING STEEL

Another part of the project that required creativity was the steel itself. In the design, the tower's legs had curved sections. It was part of what gave the tower its distinct look. But the pieces of steel had been cast straight. No one was sure how to give them the right curve.

Steelworker Bob LeBlanc had the task of figuring out how to bend the beams. He experimented and found a method that produced accurate results. To do it, LeBlanc heated one side of the beam. The side that had been heated shrank as it cooled. But the side that had not been heated did not change at all. It produced the curves that were needed.

THE TOP HOUSE

The tower continued to grow. By November it was ready for the top house. This five-story building would crown the tower. Its highlights would be a revolving restaurant and an observation deck. They would provide visitors with spectacular views of the Cascade Mountains and downtown Seattle.

PICKING A COLOR

When the steel beams arrived at the Space Needle site, they were coated in yellow primer. Designers had not yet settled on a color scheme. Many ideas were suggested, from a serious gray and white to a bold red. In the fall of 1961, the official paint colors were announced. They had space-age names to match the fair's theme. The tower would be "astronaut white" with the core in "orbital olive." The halo would sport "re-entry red," and the roof and sunburst would be "galaxy gold." The structure was painted all-white in later years, though sometimes it was painted in other colors for special occasions.

CONSTRUCTION TIMELINE

MARCH 8, 1961	The final design is approved.
APRIL 17, 1961	Work on the foundation begins.
MAY 26, 1961	Concrete is poured for the foundation.
JUNE 26, 1961	The steel crew begins work.
MID-JULY 1961	The steel core reaches 120 feet (37 m).
OCTOBER 1961	The tower reaches 500 feet (152 m).
DECEMBER 8, 1961	The gas torch is placed at the top of the tower.
JANUARY 1962	Workers begin installing the electrical system and elevators.
MARCH 1962	The Space Needle is completed.
APRIL 21, 1962	The 1962 World's Fair opens.

Construction of the Space Needle was completed in just over one year. What might have made the Space Needle faster to build than other types of buildings? Why might its builders have been motivated to finish it on schedule?

Steel workers with steady nerves worked on the top house, often without harnesses. When they completed the framing, they used the crane to install the final piece. It was a gas torch that would sit on the top house. On December 8, workers installed the gas torch. It gave the Space Needle a height of 605 feet (184 m).

The top house was framed but not completed. Before any more work could take place on it, Collop had to remove the crane from the core. A panel in the core had not been welded on purpose. Workers opened this panel and moved the crane through it. Then they lowered the crane to the ground.

More than 100 workers swarmed the top house to make sure it would be ready for the fair's opening. They installed wiring, plumbing, elevators, and kitchens. Painters finished details on the inside and outside. The entire building was completed in March. The team had built the tallest building west of the Mississippi River in only 407 days.

FURTHER EVIDENCE

Chapter Three discusses the rise of the Space Needle. Read the opinion piece at the link below. How does it support the importance of the Space Needle? Why do people feel so strongly about it? Provide some evidence to support your ideas.

THE IMPORTANCE OF SEEING THE SPACE NEEDLE

abdocorelibrary.com/engineering-space-needle

THE SPACE NEEDLE TODAY

During the six months of the 1962 World's Fair, visitors flocked to the Space Needle. More than 2.3 million people were willing to wait in lines for hours to get to the top. It was a chance to experience a bit of the future.

While the world has changed since 1962, the lure of the Space Needle has not. People are still inspired by its graceful lines. They still like to think of the future with a sense

The Space Needle remains an iconic part of Seattle's skyline.

of wonder. And people still like to marvel at the triumph of human engineering.

PROVING ITS STRENGTH

The engineering work on the Space Needle has been put to the test many times since it opened. The first major event occurred before the fair was even over. On October 12, 1962, a cyclone battered the west coast. High winds and rain blew through Seattle.

When the storm arrived, everyone in the Space Needle was

evacuated safely. The tower swayed, but it remained undamaged. Minasian had designed it to sway one inch (2.5 cm) for every 10 miles per hour (16 km/h) of wind. It performed exactly as Minasian had planned.

The next major engineering test happened just three years later. On the morning of April 29, 1965, an earthquake struck Seattle. It had a magnitude of 6.5. This is strong enough to damage or destroy buildings. But the Space Needle just swayed in a figure-eight shape. Minasian's calculations for a low center of gravity had kept the tower upright and safe.

In the next five decades, high winds and earthquakes continued to happen in Seattle. But they caused no major damage to the tower or anyone in it. The Space Needle performed well each time.

TAKING CARE OF THE NEEDLE

To stay in good shape, the Space Needle needs regular care. A ten-person crew has this daring and often dangerous job. They make repairs and replace lightbulbs on the halo and roof. When winds grow too strong, they slow or stop the elevators. If icicles form on the halo, one crew member breaks them off while another catches the icicles in a bag.

In 2008 the Space Needle received its first cleaning. A three-person cleaning crew rappelled from the top of the needle using ropes. On their way down, they sprayed the Space Needle with hot, high-pressure water. It removed the pollution, dirt, and bird droppings that had built up over more than 40 years.

The observation deck provides amazing views of the city and nearby landscapes.

CHANGING WITH THE TIMES

The Space Needle has undergone many additions and renovations since the fair. In 1982 construction on the tower's Skyline Level was completed. It included a viewing deck and restaurant located at the tower's 100-foot (30-m) mark.

In June 2000, the Space Needle reopened after a $20 million renovation. A ramp now spirals around the tower base, guiding visitors to the elevators. A new observation deck has 360-degree views without any obstructions. The restaurant has been completely made over, as have the gift shops.

Today, the Space Needle continues to point to the future. It has cutting-edge touchscreen displays on the observation deck. They offer a panorama from cameras in the tower's top. Visitors can zoom in on the display to get amazing, detailed views of Seattle.

This stunning 605-foot (184-m) tower began as a simple sketch. The structure that critics thought would be a gimmick has earned a place as a true landmark. It is a lasting symbol of Seattle, the World's Fair, and the future.

STRAIGHT TO THE
SOURCE

In 1987 the Space Needle celebrated its twenty-fifth anniversary. In honor of it, journalist Rob Carson summed up the reasons the tower had become such a large presence in Seattle:

> *The unmistakable landmark of the Space Needle provides a reference point that is not only geographical, but temporal. It stands for a brief, shining moment of optimism, firmly anchored to the soil. That's the advantage it has over all the rest of the towers in cities around the world. It not only tells us where we are, it tells us where we've been.*

> Source: Knute Berger. *Space Needle: The Spirit of Seattle.* Seattle, WA: Documentary Media, 2012. Print. 168.

What's the Big Idea?

Carson observed that the Space Needle provides a reference point in both space and time. What does that say about the engineering and design of the Space Needle? What qualities does the tower possess that have allowed it to evolve from a fair attraction to a national landmark?

FAST FACTS

- Plans for the Space Needle began when Edward Carlson drew a rough sketch of a tower.

- The Space Needle was built for the 1962 World's Fair as a symbol of life in the future.

- Victor Steinbrueck added graceful lines and a narrow waist to the Space Needle's final design.

- To lower the Space Needle's center of gravity, engineer John Minasian designed a deep, heavy foundation.

- Construction boss Paul Collop developed a new way to use a crane to get supplies to high elevations.

- Steelworker Bob LeBlanc found a process for bending the Space Needle's massive steel beams.

- The construction of the Space Needle was completed in 407 days.

- The Space Needle is 605 feet tall (184 m). It was the tallest building west of the Mississippi River when it was completed.

- More than 2.3 million people rode to the top of the Space Needle during the World's Fair.

- The Space Needle has withstood high winds and earthquakes without any major damage.

STOP AND
THINK

Say What?

Engineers and architects use language specific to designing buildings. Find five engineering or architectural terms in this book that were new to you. Use a dictionary to find their meanings and write each word in a sentence.

Another View

Many people in Seattle love the Space Needle, but not everyone may share that opinion. They may believe it disrupts the natural beauty of the surrounding mountains. Write an opinion piece for a blog that is either in favor of or against the Space Needle. Back up your opinion with three specific points.

Surprise Me

The idea for the Space Needle and its design were inspired by a variety of elements. Which element surprised you the most? Write a few sentences explaining this element and how it influenced the final design of the Space Needle.

Tell the Tale

The 1962 World's Fair focused on the future. Imagine you are planning the next World's Fair. What theme would you choose, and what type of structure would you use as a symbol? Make an elevation drawing, including a few sentences about how the structure fits into the fair's theme.

GLOSSARY

abstract
focused on the idea of
something rather than what
it's really like

architect
a person who
designs buildings

building codes
rules for constructing a
structure in a certain area

cast
to form an item, such as a
steel beam, by pouring a
liquid into a mold and letting
it cool

cyclone
a storm with heavy winds
and rain

gimmick
a trick or method used to
gain interest or business

magnitude
a measurement that
represents the strength of
an earthquake

panorama
an unbroken view of an area
in every direction

pedestal
the base of a tall building

primer
a coating put on an object
before the final paint is used

rappel
to go down a vertical face,
such as a building, using
only ropes

weld
a joint formed by heating
and cooling two pieces
of metal

ONLINE RESOURCES

To learn more about the Space Needle, visit our free resource websites below.

Visit **abdocorelibrary.com** for free Common Core resources for teachers and students, including vetted activities, multimedia, and booklinks, for deeper subject comprehension.

Visit **abdobooklinks.com** for free additional online weblinks for further learning. These links are routinely monitored and updated to provide the most current information available.

LEARN MORE

Dillon, Patrick. *The Story of Buildings: From the Pyramids to the Sydney Opera House and Beyond.* Somerville, MA: Candlewick Press, 2014.

INDEX

About the Author

Kate Conley has been writing nonfiction books for children for nearly two decades. When she's not writing, Conley spends her time reading, sewing, and solving crossword puzzles. She lives in Minnesota with her husband and two children.